Helping Children See Jesus

ISBN: 978-1-933206-24-0

THE TESTS OF TRUE FAITH
New Testament Volume 39: James

Authors: Velma Brubaker Kiefer, Mary Carson Kuschke,
Doris S. Moose
Illustrator: Vernon Henkel
Colorization courtesy of Good Life Ministries
Typesetting and Layout: Morgan Melton, Patricia Pope

© 2018 Bible Visuals International
PO Box 153, Akron, PA 17501-0153
Phone: (717) 859-1131
www.biblevisuals.org

All rights reserved. No part of this publication may be reproduced, stored in a retrieval system or transmitted in any form by any means, electronic, mechanical, photocopy, recording or otherwise, without the prior permission of the publisher, except as provided by USA copyright law.

RELATED ITEMS

To access related items (such as activities, memory verse posters and translated texts) please visit our web store at shop.biblevisuals.org and enter 1039 in the search box on the page.

FREE TEXT DOWNLOAD

To access a FREE printable copy of the teaching text (PDF format) in English or other available languages, enter S1039DL in the search box. Add the item to your cart, and use coupon code XTACSV17 at checkout. Once your order is processed you will receive an email with a link to the free download.

Faith, if it hath not works, is dead.

James 2:17a

Lesson 1
FAITH TESTED BY WORKS

NOTE TO THE TEACHER

James knew Jesus well. They lived in the same home and had the same mother, Mary. They did not have the same father. Jesus, the Son of God, was born supernaturally. James was the natural son of Joseph and Mary. So Jesus and James were half-brothers. As boys, they played together, ate together, and went together to the synagogue to worship God. We don't know exactly when James placed his trust in Jesus as Saviour. It may have been after the resurrection of Christ. (See John 7:5; 1 Corinthians 15:7.)

James speaks of himself as a servant a bondslave of God and Christ. He served as leader of the council and church in Jerusalem. (See Acts 12:17; 15:13-29; Galatians 1:19; 2:9.) James, because of his pure life and good works, was respected even by those who did not believe in Christ.

The *Epistle of James*, like all the other Bible books, is from God Himself. It contains advice on various subjects. Its theme is: Genuine faith in Christ shows itself in good works.

God teaches through the writings of Paul, that "to be justified" is to be declared righteous. That is, the person who truly trusts in Christ, is in right standing with God. Through the letter of James, God teaches that "to be justified" also means to be proved righteous. This means that a person shows others he/she is a child of God by doing good works. Works are the outcome and proof of living faith in Christ Jesus.

Depending on the ability of your students, you may wish to divide these lessons.

Before class, prepare a dummy using a bag of trash, cornstalks, pillows, or whatever is available. Use clothes like those your students wear to dress the dummy. Place it next to you with its back toward the class.

Scripture to be studied: James 1:1-27; 2:14-26; 5:10-11 and all references in outline and text.

The *aim* of the lesson: To show that true faith in Christ produces good works.

What your students should *know*: Those who belong to the Lord Jesus should do good, as He did. (See Acts 10:38.)

What your students should *feel*: A desire to show their faith by doing good works.

What your students should *do*: Determine what they can do this week that will prove they have genuine faith in the Saviour.

Lesson outline (for the teacher's and students' notebooks):
1. Faith without works is dead (James 2:17, 20, 26).
2. Genuine faith is tested by good works (James 2:21-26; Genesis 15:3-6; 22:1-14; Joshua 2:1-21; 6:25; Hebrews 11:31).
3. Real faith is tested by trials (James 5:10-11; Job 1:1-22; 38:1–41:34).
4. Tested faith is rewarded (James 1:12; Job 42:1-17).

The verse to be memorized:

Faith, if it hath not works, is dead. (James 2:17a)

THE LESSON

Who is this beside me? He hasn't moved since class began. Nor has he said a word. Who will try to get him to take part? (Give students opportunity to talk to the "person".) Why do you suppose he doesn't answer? (Guide students to the correct answer: the "person" isn't real.) We can talk to him, even shout at him. But he will never talk to us because he has no life. Do you know that it is possible to look like a Christian, even think you are a Christian, and not be a true believer in Christ? For this very reason God caused James to write a letter long ago. That letter is now part of the Word of God and is known as The Epistle of James.

1. FAITH WITHOUT WORKS IS DEAD
James 2:17, 20, 26

Show Illustration #1

Because James was giving God's message, he wrote with boldness. "Faith which does not have good works with it, is dead!" (See James 2:17, 20, 26.) It's not real faith if the person doesn't do good things for others. It is make-believe faith.

When the Lord Jesus was here on earth, He went about doing good (Acts 10:38). Just so, those who truly believe in Him prove it by doing good deeds. The person who does not do good may say he/she is a Christian. That one may dress like certain Christians. But, like the dummy, he/she is not genuine. Christ does not live within him/her.

2. GENUINE FAITH IS TESTED BY GOOD WORKS
James 2:21-26; Genesis 15:3-6; 22:1-14; Joshua 2:1-21; 6:25; Hebrews 11:31

It is important to know whether or not we are genuine Christians. In the letter of James, God tells us how we can test our faith. For example, test yourself this way: Do you believe God and obey Him? Abraham had such a test. (See James 2:21-24.) God told him to leave his comfortable home and the family he loved and go to a foreign land. "I will make of you a great nation, Abraham," God promised. "I will make your name famous." Although Abraham was 75 years old, he packed his things and left home. He did not even know where he was going! (See Hebrews 11:8.) But he obeyed. Years later, God asked Abraham for his only son, Isaac. Obediently, Abraham placed Isaac as a sacrifice on an altar. But God intervened. He was so pleased: He called Abraham His friend. And He has recorded in His Word that Abraham's obedience proved that his faith in God was genuine.

Rahab (who lived long after Abraham) had her faith tested also. She was different from Abraham. Rahab didn't know God. So she had no practice in listening to Him, trusting Him, or obeying Him. Indeed, for most of her life she had sinful thoughts and actions.

Show Illustration #2

One day two foreign spies came to Rahab's house. She knew they were her enemies because they were men who belonged to the living God of Heaven. But she let them in and hid them on the rooftop in bundles of grass. She even risked her life to keep them safe.

– 18 –

That night, crouched on the rooftop, she talked to the spies. "I know that the LORD has given our land to you and your people. We're all afraid of you. We've heard how the LORD has taken care of you.... The LORD your God, He is God in Heaven above and in earth beneath."

What did Rahab now have? (*Teacher:* Encourage discussion.) Rahab had faith in God. She believed He was exactly who He said He was: the living God of Heaven. She turned to Him, away from her old sinful ways.

Rahab begged the men, saying, "Please show me mercy. Don't destroy my family or me."

"You'll be kept safe," the spies promised.

Then Rahab hung a red rope from the window of her house high on the city wall. The spies slid down the rope to safety. Looking up, they spoke softly to Rahab. "When we come back, hang this rope out of this window. And you and your family will be spared."

And then the men tiptoed safely away. Later the spies returned with their army. They completely destroyed the city. Only those who lived in the house on the wall with the red rope hanging from the window were saved. Rahab had believed what she heard about God. She had placed her trust in Him and worked for Him by protecting two of His men. What Rahab did for them is proof that her faith in God was genuine. She had living faith. (See James 2:24-25; Hebrews 11:31.)

3. REAL FAITH IS TESTED BY TRIALS
James 5:10-11; Job 1:1-22; 38:1–41:34

There is another way you can test yourself to see if you have genuine faith in God and His Son. This is the test: Do you have joy even when trials come?

God caused James to write his letter at a time when many Christians were hated because of their faith in Christ. Some were beaten and thrown into prison. Others were murdered.

They had ordinary trials also. They became sick; had accidents; some had money troubles; others didn't have enough to eat. But God commanded, "Be full of joy when you have all kinds of trials" (James 1:2). How could they do this? How can you do this? It's not fun to feel pain. You're not happy if you are hungry. It's not nice to hear someone laugh at you, saying, "Ha, ha! He's a Christian." But in such trials you prove whether or not you have genuine faith in God.

In his letter, James mentions another person, Job, who had lived long, long ago. He was a rich man who belonged to God. (See Job 1:8.) But God allowed Job's faith in Him to be tested. This is what happened:

One day a servant rushed to Job crying, "Some raiders stole all your oxen and donkeys! They killed all your farmhands except me. I am the only one left."

Show Illustration #3

Immediately another messenger, rubbing his smoke-filled eyes, ran in with more bad news: "The fire of God has fallen from Heaven! It burned up all your sheep and all your shepherds. I am the only one who escaped!"

Before this man finished, another dashed up to Job. "Three gangs of men have stolen all your camels! They killed your servants! I alone have escaped."

While he was still speaking, another ran to Job exclaiming, "A mighty wind swept in from the desert. Your house collapsed. And all your children are dead!"

Job was sad indeed when he lost so much that was precious to him. But he fell down on the ground and worshiped God. "All these things were gifts from You, God," Job said. "So You have the right to take them away. Blessed be the name of the Lord." And the Bible tells us, in all of this, Job did not sin or speak unkindly against God.

Then things became worse. Job became sick. He had pain day and night. His wife said ugly things about Job and God. Bit Job kept on trusting God completely.

But after trusting God for a long time, Job lost his patience. He begged God to let him die, so that his suffering could be ended. When God did not let him die, he became angry.

Then God spoke to Job right out of a whirlwind. "Where were you when I formed the earth and brought the sea under control?" God asked. "Can you cause the morning to appear, Job? Do you know anything about the deep places of the earth? Where do light and darkness come from? What do you know about the storehouses of snow and hail? Can you make rain and ice? Do you know anything about the movement of the stars? Can you make lightning strike? Can you control the wild animals?"

How ashamed Job was! He remembered God can do whatever He wants. He has the right to test His own people. Through the trials, God wanted to teach Job to trust Him patiently. Finally Job learned his lesson and asked God's forgiveness.

4. TESTED FAITH IS REWARDED
James 1:12; Job 42:1-17

God, who knows all things, knew that Job was genuinely sorry for the wrong things he had said and done. He forgave Job and immediately spoke of him four times as "My servant." (See Job 42:7-8.) Job also prayed for his three friends who had been harsh and unkind to him. When he did this, the Lord healed him and gave him great happiness. (See Job 42:10.)

Show Illustration #4

Job's brothers, sisters and former friends came and ate with him. They told him how sorry they were about all his trials. They even brought gifts of money and gold. And the Lord blessed Job with twice as much as he had before!

If Job could speak to us today, he would probably say exactly what James wrote in his letter. "Blessed [happy] is the man who endures testings. For when he is tried, he will receive the crown of life, which the Lord has promised to those who love Him." (See James 1:12; compare Hebrews 12:11.)

Good works are extremely important. Every Christian believer should be busy doing good. But if you have never placed your trust in the Lord Jesus, good works have no value at all. Giving food to the poor is good. (*Teacher:* Name "good works" familiar to your students.) But this will never forgive your sins or prepare you for Heaven. You must be born into God's family by receiving His Son as your Saviour from sin.

Do you have true faith? Do you obey God as Abraham did? Do you, like Rahab, help others who belong to God? Do you have joy when trials come (as Job did at first)? Do you pray for those who are unkind to you, as Job did?

Will you list in your notebook what you can do this week to prove to yourself that you have genuine faith in God the Son?

Lesson 2
TRUE FAITH AND OTHERS

NOTE TO THE TEACHER

Through James, God addresses all believers: rich and poor, important and the unnoticed. He reminds us that all who are born again are brothers in Christ. He adds, "Do not say you are a Christian if you do not act like one." The sin particularly mentioned is "respect of persons." That is, we are not to love and honor people because they are rich or famous. We are to love all people equally. (*Teacher:* Examine your own life. Do you show partiality? If so, you may not be genuinely born again. You say you have faith in Christ. But if you are unkind to the poor or unlovely, your faith in Christ may not be real.)

Devoted service for others is the outcome and proof of faith. This is what God says to us through the little letter of James. Help your students to examine themselves to make certain they have true faith. (See 1 Corinthians 13:5.) May their works give outward evidence that they are truly saved.

For the opening object lesson, use a solid silver coin and a make-believe coin. If one is not available, or if coins are not used in your culture, use another pair of objects.

Scripture to be studied: James 2:1-20; Luke 18:18-24; Ruth 1:1–4:22

The *aim* of the lesson: To make plain that those who have true faith in Christ are loving, kind and helpful even, to the most unlovely.

What your students should *know*: If they are not kind or helpful toward others, they probably do not have genuine faith in Christ.

What your students should *feel*: An earnest desire to have genuine faith.

What your students should *do*:
  Unsaved: Receive the Lord Jesus as Saviour from sin.
  Saved: Determine how and to whom they can show love, kindness and helpfulness this week.

Lesson outline (for the teacher's and students' notebooks):
1. True faith is kind to all types of people (James 2:1-5, 9).
2. True faith loves others (James 2:8, 12).
3. True faith helps others (James 2:14-16).
4. True faith takes care of others (James 1:27; 2:14-17).

The verse to be memorized:
Faith, if it hath not works, is dead. (James 2:17a)

THE LESSON

Here in my hand are two coins. One is genuine. The other is not. How can you tell the difference? (*Teacher:* Use any familiar object which your students know how to test.) The real coin rings when it is dropped on glass or metal. The make-believe coin lands with a dull thud. The genuine coin is solid and cannot be bent. The other one bends quite easily. (Allow your students to make the tests as they discuss the differences between the real and the imitation.)

Everyone who says he/she has trusted in Christ can test to see if his/her faith is genuine. To have imitation faith is extremely serious. For in some future day, each of us will stand before the Lord. If your faith in Christ is not real, He'll say to you, "Depart from Me. I never knew you." (See Matthew 7:23; 25:41-46.) And you will be separated from God forever and ever.

In the letter which James wrote, God tells us how to test ourselves. He says, "Faith without works is dead." So if you're not doing good works, then perhaps you're not a real Christian.

1. TRUE FAITH IS KIND TO ALL TYPES OF PEOPLE
James 2:1-5, 9

Are you wondering what kind of "good works" God has in mind? There are several. For example: how do you treat poor people? This is a good test of your faith in Christ.

Show Illustration #5

"Do you look on one person as more important than another?" God asks.

"Suppose a man comes to your meeting wearing a gold ring and good clothes. At the same time a poor man comes in old clothes. Do you show respect to the person in nice clothes and say, 'Come, sit in this good place?' Do you say to the poor man, 'Stand up over there?' Or, 'Sit on the floor by my feet?' Are you thinking, 'This rich man is more important than the poor man. Such thinking is sinful.' This is God's Word.

When you see someone who is lame, do you help that person or laugh at him/her? Do you treat others as the Lord Jesus did? According to this test, do you have genuine faith in Christ?

2. TRUE FAITH LOVES OTHERS
James 2:8, 12

When the Lord Jesus was here on earth, He tested a rich man who had much authority. The man did the best he knew to obey God's Law. He wanted to be certain of getting to Heaven some day. But down deep inside he had questions which troubled him. *Do I really have eternal life?* he wondered. *Who can tell me how to go to Heaven?*

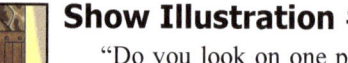

Show Illustration #6

When the Lord Jesus came to his village the rich man pushed through the crowd. "Good Teacher," he began, "what good thing shall I do to get eternal life?"

Jesus replied, "You know the commandments of God: 'Do not worship any god but Me; do not steal; do not lie; honor your father and mother; love your neighbor as yourself.'"

The man replied, "Master, I have obeyed all of these laws since I was young. What else must I do?"

The Lord Jesus, God the Son, knows all things. He knew everything about the man. Speaking kindly Jesus said, "You lack one thing. Go, sell all that you have. Give your money to the poor . . . Take up your cross and follow Me."

The man said he'd kept all the commandments. He said he loved his neighbor as himself. But give all his money to his poor neighbor? That was too much.

He thought he loved God with all his heart. He didn't understand that loving the poor and sharing with them was really giving to God the Son. (See Matthew 25:34-40.)

– 20 –

Sadly, the young ruler, because he had great riches, turned away from Jesus. He felt that he worshiped the living God of Heaven. Instead, his money was his god! Because this was so, he did not have real, living faith. He kept his riches for himself.

He went away without eternal life. Poor, poor rich man!

What about you? Have you truly turned to the Lord Jesus for forgiveness of sin? If so, do you truly love others? (See John 13:34-35.) Do you share what you have with others? This is another test of genuine faith. (See 1 John 3:17-18.)

3. TRUE FAITH HELPS OTHERS
James 2:14-16

In the letter of James, God mentions another way to test whether or not we have real, true faith in Him. He says, "Your faith is lifeless if you talk about being a believer in Christ, but never do good works to show it. Suppose a Christian does not have clothes or food. You say to him, 'Good-bye. Keep yourself warm. Eat well.' That is not what it means to have real faith in Christ. You must act out your faith by helping him in whatever way you can."

Those who received God's message through James would have thought of the helpful man, Boaz.

Boaz lived hundreds of years earlier. He was an important man in the city of Bethlehem. He worshiped the true God of Heaven. Boaz was rich and had many people working for him. He spoke to them courteously and wished them God's blessings. Even though they were below him in importance, he was kind to them.

One day the people of Bethlehem saw a tired-looking woman and a young lady approaching the city. The people wondered and whispered about the two. The older woman was Naomi. The younger was Ruth. Ten years before, Naomi and her family had left Bethlehem to live in Moab. There her husband and two sons died. Now she was coming home. And Ruth, her daughter-in-law, had chosen to come along with Naomi. Both women were very poor.

In those days it was the custom for the owners of fields to help poor people get enough food. They told their workers to leave some of the grain on the ground around the edges of the field. Poor people understood that they were allowed to come in and gather this grain free.

Show Illustration #7

Since Ruth and Naomi were poor, Ruth went to pick up the leftover grain in Boaz's field.

One day Boaz came to talk to his workers. He saw Ruth and asked, "Who is that picking up grain over there?"

"She is Ruth, who came from Moab with Naomi."

Now immediately upon hearing *Moab*, Boaz could have become angry. The Moabites were enemies of the Israelites. And Boaz was an Israelite. The Moabites fought against the people of Israel, and worshiped false gods.

4. TRUE FAITH TAKES CARE OF OTHERS
James 1:27; 2:14-17

But Boas showed great kindness to the young widow, Ruth. He felt sorry for her and admired her for choosing to stay with Naomi. He was glad that she had turned from the false, make-believe Moabite gods to worship the true and living God of Heaven. Boaz didn't think of Ruth as a poor person who was far below him. He knew she was someone who needed help.

Imagine Ruth's surprise when Boaz came to her!

Show Illustration #8

"You will be safe here," he promised her. "Stay with the other women who work for me. Pick up all the grain you want. When you are thirsty, you may have some of our water. And you may eat with us at mealtime."

"Thank you, sir!" Ruth exclaimed, bowing before him. "Thank you, oh so much!"

Boaz turned and spoke secretly to his men. "Drop some extra grain on purpose so Ruth will be able to get more," he commanded.

Boaz did more than talk about his faith in God. By taking care of Ruth and Naomi, he showed his faith was real.

*I need a volunteer to come stand by me for a few minutes. (*Teacher:* If no one responds, select a student who is not shy. Exchange greetings with him/her. At the same time, drop this book on the floor for him/her to pick up.)

Would you say the student is alive or dead? Are you certain? If he/she had been lying perfectly still on the floor with his/her eyes tightly closed, would you have been just as certain?

How can you tell the student has life? (*Teacher:* Encourage student participation.) He/she heard what I said; walked to the front and picked up the book. In other words, he/she acts very much alive.

Now there are many people who say they are Christians. But they do not act like Christians. God's Word says that born again believers are to be kind to all types of people, no matter how poor or unlovely they may be. They are to love others and help them. They are to take care of others. If they don't, it may be that they don't have genuine, living faith in the Lord Jesus. If our friend here didn't move at all, you would wonder if he/she is alive. And if you are not living as a Christian should, then perhaps you don't have eternal life.

There is the possibility that you really are a child of God. You are perfectly certain of it. But perhaps you did not know that God requires you to do good works after you are saved. Now, however, you know. So what are you going to do?

Will you list in your notebook the names of those who are poor or unlovely people you have been ignoring? Write exactly how you plan to express kindness to them. Do you know someone who needs help? Add the name to the list in your notebook. Determine and write down now how you plan to help that person. Do you know someone who needs the kind of care you can give? Caring for others does not cost money. It may take time. Are you willing to care for that person today? This week? How will you do it? Mention that in your notebook.

There is something you must know. It is quite possible to be genuinely nice and do good works without being a true child of God. Indeed, there are many who think that because they do many good things, God will save them. The devil likes to have people believe that. But it is not true. Doing good does not save anyone. There is only one way to become a member of the family of God. You must know that the Lord Jesus Christ is the Son of God. You must believe that He, the perfect One, took the punishment of your sin when He died on the cross. When you tell Him you are sorry for your sin and ask His forgiveness, He will forgive you. Will you receive the Lord Jesus Christ as your Saviour from sin right now?

* As suggested by Dr. Charles C. Ryrie in his book: *Easy-to-give Object Lessons.* Copyright 1974. Moody Press, Moody Bible Institute of Chicago. Used by permission.

Lesson 3
GENUINE FAITH AND THE TONGUE

> **NOTE TO THE TEACHER**
>
> The purpose of The Epistle of James is to show how genuine Christian faith is to be lived. In lesson #1, we saw that the reality of our faith is proved through the testings and trials which come to us. From the second lesson, we understand that our attitude toward others prove whether or not we have genuine faith. In this third lesson, we learn how practical the Christian life is. For it is the tongue under control that reveals true living faith in Christ.
>
> Misuse of the tongue means a dwarfed life (James 3:1-5). James puts the utmost importance on proper speech for a truly spiritual life. For, he says, although we all oftentimes offend, the most frequent offense comes from the tongue. So, one who is victorious over these sins may be said to be mature. On the other hand, he who sins in speech is dwarfed in his spiritual development (compare Matthew 5:34-37, 48). Control of speech will include control of the entire body just as bits control horses, rudders control ships or a small spark sets a forest fire.
>
> Misuse of the tongue means a defiled life (James 3:6-8). The misused tongue will reveal inner defilement and sin.
>
> Misuse of the tongue means a deceitful life (James 3:9-12). When the tongue, which should be used to bless God curse man, the words *deceit* and *hypocrisy* gives James's description of such a person.
>
> This lesson on the tongue is extremely important!

Scripture to be studied: James 3:1-18 and all references mentioned in the lesson.

The *aim* of the lesson: To explain the necessity of asking God to control their tongues, so that what they say will prove that their faith in Christ is genuine.

What your students should *know*: They must have the help of the Lord in order to tame their tongues.

What your students should *feel*: Ashamed that they use their tongues carelessly.

What your students should *do*: Ask the Lord today (and every day) to "keep the door of their lips." Determine how their controlled tongues can honor Him today, this week.

Lesson outline (for the teacher's and students' notebooks):

1. A wild tongue can destroy good things (James 3:5-8; 1 Samuel 17:1-18:30; 20:1–21:9).
2. The tongue can say good things and bad at almost the same time (James 3:8-12; Matthew 26:57-75; Mark 14:53-72; Luke 22:54-62; John 18:12-27).
3. God's Word says the tongue has great power (James 3:3-5).
4. There is a difference between genuine faith and the tongue (James 3:13-18).

The verse to be memorized:

Faith, if it hath not works, is dead. (James 2:17a)

THE LESSON

Have you ever tried to tame a wild animal? Or have you watched someone else do it? Men work for months to tame tigers. (*Teacher:* Name an animal familiar to your students.)

God says (in the letter which James wrote) that men have been able to tame animals, birds, serpents, and creatures of the sea. But there is something which no one can tame by himself. This wild, little thing causes everyone everywhere all kinds of trouble. What is so wild and untamable? It is the tongue, which is only a tiny part of the body. But with it words are formed. And some words can cause great harm.

1. A WILD TONGUE CAN DESTROY GOOD THINGS
James 3:5-8; 1 Samuel 17:1-18:30; 20:1–21:9

"The tongue is like a fire set by the devil," the Bible teaches.

Suppose you say to someone angrily, "I hate you!" Does that hurt his/her feelings? If you tell a lie about a person, does it help or harm him/her? (*Teacher:* Encourage group discussion about the misuse of the tongue.) The tongue seems quite unimportant. But like wildfire, it can cause all kinds of trouble.

David (though he lived hundreds of years before James wrote his letter) discovered how hard it is to control the tongue.

When David was young, he surprised everyone by killing the wicked giant Goliath. King Saul was so pleased that he placed David in command of the army. The people were delighted when they learned of David's killing the giant. They ran into the streets, singing, playing musical instruments and dancing happily. The women cheered, saying, "Saul has slain thousands! And David has slain ten thousands!"

This made King Saul wildly angry. "Next they will make David king in my place!" Saul exclaimed jealously. He watched David serving God and the people. He saw how God blessed David. He realized how popular David was with the people. And Saul's jealousy turned to fierce hatred. One day he announced to his men, "David must be killed!"

When David learned this, he knew he had to escape at once. *Where shall I go?* he wondered. Alas, he didn't ask the Lord to show him what to do. Instead, he rushed to the city of Nob where the tabernacle (the house of God) stood. Ahimelech, the priest of God, and other priests lived in Nob.

Show Illustration #9

Ahimelech was surprised to see David without any of the soldiers who were under his command. "Why did you come alone?" Ahimelech asked.

"The king sent me on secret business," David lied. "He told me not to tell anyone why I'm here. I 've told my men to meet me later. Now, what is there to eat? Give me five loaves of bread, or anything else you can."

"I do not have any ordinary bread," Ahimelech replied. "There is only the holy bread from the table in the house of God. That is the bread which only the priests may eat."

Ahimelech hesitated to give David the holy bread. But since David was hungry, Ahimelech got him five loaves.

While the two men were talking, David saw from the corner of his eye King Saul's chief herdsman. David was terrified. *He will tell Saul where I am. I must get out of here,* he decided.

Turning to Ahimelech, David asked smoothly, "Do you have a sword or spear I could borrow? I was in such a hurry to do the king's business, I forgot to get my sword," David lied.

– 22 –

Ahimelech answered, "The only sword I have is Goliath's. It's the sword you took from him the day you killed him. You may have it."

David was delighted. "There is no sword like this one," he said, and left quickly. He fled to an enemy's country, hoping to hide there. But people saw him and knew who he was. So he ran for his life again. This time he hid in caves and forests.

One day he received dreadful news. Ahimelech's son staggered into David's camp. His face was filled with terror. His clothes were torn. Trembling, he gasped, "King Saul has killed everyone in the city: my father, all the other priests, the men, women, children, even the animals!"

David shuddered. He knew exactly what had happened. The herdsman who saw him with Ahimelech reported him to King Saul. The king was wild with rage because David was running away from him. He was furious at Ahimelech for not telling on David. In his rage, Saul ordered his men to kill Ahimelech and everyone else in the city.

David was horrified and ashamed. He had lied to Ahimelech. Because of his lies everyone in Nob was dead. "This is all my fault," he groaned.

Turning to God, David cried, 'O Lord, forgive the sin of my tongue." He was truly sorry for his lies. Later he wrote a prayer for his tongue: "O Lord, set a guard before my mouth. Keep watch over the door of my lips" (Psalm 141:3).

Has something or someone been destroyed because of your tongue? If so, have you asked God's forgiveness?

2. THE TONGUE CAN SAY GOOD THINGS AND BAD AT ALMOST THE SAME TIME
James 3:8-12; Matthew 26:57-75; Mark 14:53-72; Luke 22:54-62; John 18:12-27

God says more about the tongue in James's letter. He says it doesn't speak the same way all the time. "Sometimes it praises God. Sometimes it curses men who are made like God. Blessing and cursing come out of the same mouth. This is not right! Does a fountain [spring] have both salt water and fresh water? Can you pick olives from a fig tree? Or figs from a grape vine? No!" (See James 3:8-12.) Such things don't happen in nature. Yet strangely enough the tongue acts this way. God says this should never happen. Peter, one of the disciples of Jesus, knew how undependable the tongue is. If Peter could be here today, perhaps he would tell us about it this way:

Show Illustration #10

"I, Peter, thought I was strong and brave. I boasted about my love for the Lord. I always spoke up quickly when He asked us a question. I was the one who said to Him, 'You are the Christ, the Son of the living God.' My tongue blessed and praised Him.

"Then one night, we walked with Jesus to a garden where He wanted to pray. Sadly, the Lord told us, 'This night all of you will run away and leave Me.'

"Immediately I said, 'Not I! Even if everyone else runs off, I won't!'

"The Lord sighed, saying, 'Peter, before morning comes, you will have turned against Me three times.' 'Even if I have to die for You, I will never turn against You,' I insisted. I was very sure of myself.

"Shortly a mob carrying torches rushed into the garden. There were soldiers with swords. At first I tried to fight. But Jesus told me to stop. I became terribly frightened. Afraid that they might make me a prisoner, I ran and hid. John and I watched as the men led Jesus away to be questioned. We followed at a safe distance.

"John slipped into a courtyard where he knew the servant girl. I followed, hoping no one would see me in the dark. The girl looked at me closely. 'Are you one of Jesus' disciples?' she asked. 'I am not!' I answered sharply. (I got away from her so she wouldn't speak to me again.)

"I was shivering and moved toward a fire to keep warm. Another girl looked at me. 'This man was with Jesus,' she announced. Everyone stared at me. I was afraid. 'I don't even know the man!' I lied with a curse. My heart pounding with fear, I moved away from the firelight. Later I moved toward the fire again. A man spoke this time. 'I saw you in the garden with Jesus.' I cursed and answered, 'I don't know what you're talking about. I don't know Him!'

"Just then Jesus came out of the room where He had been questioned. He looked down at me sadly. I remembered what He had told me. I wished I could take back my words. My tongue had once honored Him by saying, 'You are the Son of God.' Now the same tongue had cursed and said, 'I do not know Him.' Oh, how ashamed I was!"

The experiences of David and Peter prove that the tongue is wild and hard to control. But there is more.

3. GOD'S WORD SAYS THE TONGUE HAS GREAT POWER
James 3:3-5

Show Illustration #11

"If you want to control a horse and guide it you put a bridle on it. The bridle has a bit–a little piece of metal which fits in the horse's mouth. When you pull it toward you, though it is tiny, it hurts the horse's mouth. So this little thing can control even the largest horse. In the same way, a small piece of metal (called a rudder) turns a huge ship even in a strong wind." (See James 3:3-4.) Just so, the tongue, though it is a tiny part of the body, is powerful indeed. It can cause either good or evil.

4. THERE IS A DIFFERENCE BETWEEN GENUINE FAITH AND THE TONGUE
James 3:13-18

There are people whose tongues are never under control. They speak unkindly of others. They complain about almost anything and everything. They tell lies. They curse. Are such people in the family of God? Probably not. (See James 1:26.) If your tongue is out of control most of the time, check on yourself right now. Ask God's forgiveness for your sin. Turn to the Lord Jesus and receive Him as your Saviour this very moment.

Perhaps you are perfectly certain that you have already placed all your trust in the Lord. You know you are His child. Yet there are times when your tongue is loose and runs wild. You hate yourself for the things you say. David and Peter hated themselves too. They learned this very important lesson: no one can tame or control his/her tongue by himself/herself. But God can and will help you to control it if you ask His help.

Show Illustration #12

Remember what David prayed? "O Lord, set a guard before my mouth. Keep watch over the door of my lips." If you are a child of God, will you pray that right now?

If your tongue is under the control of God this week, you will have all kinds of opportunities to use it for Him. List in your notebook the places you will be able to speak His praises. Mention the names of those to whom you can speak of His love. Name those who need to hear kind and helpful words from you.

Words that please God are wonderful proofs that you have genuine, living faith in the Lord Jesus Christ. Will you let Him control you and your tongue?

Lesson 4
LIVING FAITH AND SELFISHNESS

Scripture to be studied: James 4:1-7; 2 Samuel 11:1–12:23; Luke 12:16-21

The *aim* of the lesson: To show the danger and results of living selfishly and the importance of submitting to the Lord.

What your students should *know*: That by nature we are all selfish and self-willed.

What your students should *feel*: Hatred for selfishness.

What your students should *do*: Confess their selfish acts to God immediately. Determine what habits must be changed so they can live unselfishly.

Lesson outline (for the teacher's and students' notebooks):

1. A selfish person wants things only for himself. (James 4:1-4).
2. Trying to make yourself seem better than others is selfishness (James 4:11-12; 5:9; 2 Samuel 11:1–12:23).
3. Doing what you want to do, instead of doing what God wills, is selfishness (James 4:13-15; Luke 12:16-21).
4. Victory over selfishness can be realized (James 4:6-10).

The verse to be memorized:

Faith, if it hath not works, is dead. (James 2:17a)

NOTE TO THE TEACHER

It is God's purpose that each Christian believer should be mature, full-grown. (See Matthew 5:48; Ephesians 4:13; 2 Peter 3:18.)

Therefore, each believer should have as his/her goal full development in the Christian life. A test is a tool for helping attain this goal. From the book of James we learn how to test ourselves.

This lesson deals with the cause of most of our problems: self and selfish desires. Pray that you and your students will know the joy of full surrender to Christ the Lord.

THE LESSON

Have you seen a parade? A religious procession? A fiesta? (*Teacher:* Name an event familiar to your group.) Suppose someone else with a banner crowds in ahead of the flag bearer (or the statue, or the one in costume). Shouting, "**Me First!**" he pushes and shoves, waving his arms wildly. On his flag are the same two words: **Me First**. What would you think of such a person? (*Teacher:* Allow response, leading to the idea of selfishness.)

Have you ever had the feeling: **Me First**? Suppose someone would bring us a huge box of _____ . (*Teacher:* Name something your students long to have.) He unloads the carton, saying, "These are for you. Help yourself!" Maybe there is only one that is your favorite color. Would you grab for it? Or would you wait quietly, letting others choose first? Even though a grabber may not say a word, everyone knows he is a **Me First** person.

Suppose we decided to have an outing. One says, "I think we should have it at _____." (*Teacher:* In each case, name a place your students like to go.) Another says, "I think _____ is nicer."

You say, "The best place to go is _____. I refuse to go anywhere else." If you are like this, you are a **Me First** person. And a **Me First** person is a selfish person.

Selfishness is not new. The Jewish Christians, to whom James addressed his letter, had the same problem. Even though they were children of God, they loved themselves more than they loved others. Alas, many of us are exactly the same way. So the Holy Spirit of God has much to teach us through *The Epistle of James*.

1. A SELFISH PERSON WANTS THINGS ONLY FOR HIMSELF
James 4:1-4

Show Illustration #13

God says, "What starts wars and fights among you? Is it not because you want many things and are fighting to have them? You want something you do not have, so you kill. You want something but cannot get it, so you fight for it. You do not get things because you do not ask God for them. Or if you do ask, you do not receive because your reasons for asking are wrong. You want these things only to please yourself" (James 4:1-3, The New Life Testament).

Do you know anyone who is always wishing for something more for himself/herself? Is that person happy after getting what he/she wants? (Students should discuss this, teacher.)

David (whom we studied in our last lesson) later became king. Like most kings, he had the best of everything. Alas, he wanted something he should not have had. And he wanted it very, very much. King David wanted a woman named Bathsheba. He loved her and wanted to marry her. But Bathsheba was already married to someone else–Uriah, a soldier.

More than anything, David wanted beautiful Bathsheba to be his wife. He thought, What can I do? How can I get her for myself? Then he had an evil idea: If Uriah would die, I could marry Bathsheba, So King David sent a command to his general, saying: "When the men are fighting, put Uriah in the front line. There he will die."

The general followed David's order. And sure enough, Uriah was killed.

Bathsheba cried for many days. In time, however, she said 'yes' to David and became his wife.

Now King David had what he wanted. But he wasn't happy after all! He couldn't forget his wickedness. He was guilty of planning the death of Uriah so Bathsheba could be his wife. Now he realized that getting what he wanted didn't make him truly happy. And the Lord was very displeased with what David had done (2 Samuel 11:27b).

The time came when David was genuinely sorry for his sins. He asked God to forgive him. In agony, he prayed: "O loving and kind God, have mercy. Have pity upon me and take away the awful stain of my sin. Oh wash me, cleanse me from this guilt. Let me be pure again. I admit my shameful deed; it haunts me day and night. It's against You and You alone I sinned and did this terrible thing. Sprinkle me with cleansing blood and I will be clean again. Wash me and I'll be whiter than snow. After You've punished me, give me back my joy again. Create in me a new, clean heart, O God, filled with clean thoughts and right desires. Restore to me again the joy of Your salvation, and make me willing to obey You." (See Psalm 51:1-12, The Living Bible.)

God forgave David's great sin, for He knew David was truly sorry. David was not put to death because of his selfishness. But there were sad results of David's sin. Uriah lay cold and dead. He could never come back to life again. And the baby son born to David and Bathsheba became deathly sick. David begged God to spare the child. He went without food and lay on the bare earth all night, praying to the Lord for the baby. Alas, a week later his son died. David's sin had been forgiven. But it didn't go unpunished. (See Hebrews 12:9-11.) Which is better: (1) to be content with God's ways? Or (2) to scheme for our own selfish desires?

2. TRYING TO MAKE YOURSELF SEEM BETTER THAN OTHERS IS SELFISHNESS
James 4:11-12; 5:9; 2 Samuel 11:1–12:23

Show Illustration #14

Do you ever talk unkindly about others? Exactly why do you do this? (*Teacher:* Encourage discussion.) Often we criticize others because we feel we are better or more important than they are.

When the Lord Jesus was on earth, He told of a Pharisee who criticized another. He spoke his criticism to God. Imagine that! Pharisees were important rulers of the Jewish people. They studied the laws of God carefully and even added extra laws of their own. Because the Pharisees lived strict lives, they were given important seats at feasts and in the synagogues where the Jews worshiped. They prayed long prayers in the temple. (See Matthew 23:14.) What did God think of their prayers? Listen!

Jesus said two men went up to the temple to pray. One was a Pharisee. The other was a publican (a tax collector). The Pharisee walked proudly to a spot where everyone could see him. Seeing the tax collector, he thought to himself, What a cheater he is! He shouldn't come into this temple of God. God will never hear his prayer!

Then, thinking of his own goodness and hating those around him, the Pharisee lifted his head and prayed: "God, I thank You that I'm not like other men. I'm not greedy, dishonest, impure, or even like that tax collector! I go without food twice a week. (That was more than the law required!) I give to God a tenth part of all that I have."

The Pharisee had finished his prayer. But had he really prayed? No, he simply told God how good he was. And he criticized the tax collector. Why? Because he was selfish. He wanted people to think he was more important than others.

Jesus said harsh words about the proud Pharisee. "Whoever makes himself seem more important than he is, will learn how little he is worth." (See Luke 18:14.)

In James, God repeated this same truth. "Do not talk against anyone or speak bad things about others . . . . Only God knows what is right or wrong. (He alone knows what is deep inside a person's heart.) . . . . The great Judge is coming." Let Him, the perfect One, do whatever criticizing must be done. (See James 4:11-12; 5:9.)

3. DOING WHAT YOU WANT TO DO, INSTEAD OF DOING WHAT GOD WILLS, IS SELFISHNESS
James 4:13-15; Luke 12:16-21

Many Christians today (as in the time of James) make selfish decisions. We like to decide what we want to do with our own lives. We think we know what is best for us. We act as if we don't need the Lord's help. Choosing what we ourselves want to do, instead of doing what God wants, is selfishness. And a selfish person is foolish indeed.

Jesus told about a selfish rich man who did what he wanted.

Show Illustration #15

The man had a large farm and good crops every year. He had plenty for himself. He had plenty to sell for extra money. But he was never quite satisfied. He wanted more and more. God continued to send sunshine and rain and good crops. The rich farmer harvested more than ever. This is wonderful! he thought. And it is all mine.

He stuffed his barns full of grain. Finally they couldn't hold any more. He could have given his extra grain to poor people. Instead, he decided to build bigger and better barns. This way he could keep everything for himself. He thought, *Soon I'll be able to take life easy. I can eat and drink and have a good time.* He went to bed feeling very good about himself and his riches.

That night something startled him. God spoke: "You foolish man! Tonight you will die. What good will your barns and your money be to you then?"

The rich man trembled! Suddenly he realized that God really controls everything, even death. That night he died, just as God had said. And he lost everything: the barns, the money, all he had. Worst of all, he lost his soul also. Foolish, selfish man!

If only he had asked God to show him how to plan. If only he had asked God to control his life. If only he had shared with others what God had given him. How differently his life might have ended.

Have you, like King David, had selfish desires? Have you wanted things only for yourself? Have you, like the Pharisee, spoken critically of others? Have you, like the land owner, chosen to do what you want instead of the will of God? If so, you are selfish. You may have placed all your trust in the Lord Jesus Christ. Your faith in Him may be genuine. But even the true child of God can be selfish. Selfishness is sin and should be confessed!

4. VICTORY OVER SELFISHNESS
James 4:6-10

God understands that life is like a war. Christian believers are in the army of God. There are enemies to be fought. The Lord Jesus Christ is the Captain of God's army. (See Hebrews 2:8.) And when He is allowed to be in control, He wins every battle.

Show Illustration #16

Will you let Him control your life? If so:

1. Tell the Lord Jesus about your selfishness. Let Him know how sorry you are for your sins. Ask Him to forgive you. (See Proverbs 28:13; 1 John 1:9.)
2. Give (submit) yourself to God. Tell Him that by yourself you cannot win

    the battle. (See Proverbs 3:34; James 4:6-7a, 10; 1 Peter 5:5b.)
3. Stand against (resist) the devil. Turn your back to him. If you do this, God promises that the devil "will run away from you." (See James 4:7b.)
4. Draw close to God and He will draw close to you (James 4:8a). By so doing you can have victory over selfishness. Each time you win a battle others, will see that you have genuine faith in the Saviour.

List in your notebook some examples of your selfishness. Mention exactly what you can do this week to have victory over selfish habits.

www.ingramcontent.com/pod-product-compliance
Lightning Source LLC
Chambersburg PA
CBHW060806090426
42736CB00002B/178